W9-BWC-839

READ MORE

Duling, Kaitlyn. *Safety in Extreme Climates.* Minneapolis: Jump!, Inc., 2020.

Grunbaum, Mara. *The Greenhouse Effect.* New York: Children's Press, an imprint of Scholastic Inc.: 2020.

Lawrence, Ellen. *What Is Climate?* New York: Bearport Publishing, 2018.

INTERNET SITES

Climate Types for Kids
www.climatetypesforkids.com

NASA/Climate Kids
climatekids.nasa.gov/menu/big-questions/

National Geographic Kids/Climate Change
kids.nationalgeographic.com/explore/science/climate-change/

INDEX

Exploring SPACE with an Astronaut

Patricia J. Murphy

Enslow Publishers, Inc.

40 Industrial Road	PO Box 38
Box 398	Aldershot
Berkeley Heights, NJ 07922	Hants GU12 6BP
USA	UK

http://www.enslow.com

Contents

Words to Know

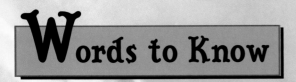

astronaut (AS troh nawt)—A person who goes into space.

black hole—A place in space with very strong gravity. Black holes can even pull in light and hold it down.

experiment (ek SPER ih ment)—A test done by scientists.

gravity (GRAV ih tee)—A force that pulls things toward larger things. Earth's gravity keeps people and other things on the ground.

space shuttle (SPAYSS SHUHT uhl)—A spacecraft used to take astronauts to space and back to Earth.

telescope (TEL e skohp)—A tool that makes objects look larger.

universe (YOO nih vurss)—Everything in space. The universe is the stars, planets, and everything else.

3 . . . 2 . . . 1 . . . Lift-off!

A space shuttle climbs high into the sky. Inside the shuttle, astronauts are on their way to learn more about space.

3

An astronaut is a
person who goes
into space.
Astronauts fly on a
space shuttle.

The space shuttle takes off like a rocket.
It lands like an airplane.

United States

Eileen Collins is an astronaut. She was the first woman to be a space shuttle pilot. She was also the first woman to be the leader of a space shuttle trip.

6

She and four other astronauts
worked as a team. Some
astronauts flew the space shuttle.
Others did experiments.

In the space shuttle, astronauts float everywhere. Sleeping bags are tied to walls. Toilets have a type of seat belt.

8

Astronauts exercise to
stay strong. They
take sponge baths to
keep clean.

Why do astronauts go into space? **✳❋✳❋**

Astronauts test ways to live and work in a world that is very different from Earth. In space, there is no up and down, no air, and the sun always shines.

Astronauts do experiments. They look
for problems and fix them. This will
make space travel safer.

What tools do astronauts use? ✳✳✳✳✳✳✳

A space shuttle is a giant toolbox!
It holds tools, like computers that
help fly the space shuttle.

space
suit

robot
arm

Astronauts use robot arms
to move things and people
outside the shuttle. On
space walks, space suits
keep astronauts safe.

13

Eileen Collins and her crew had a special job to do. They took an X-ray telescope into space with them.

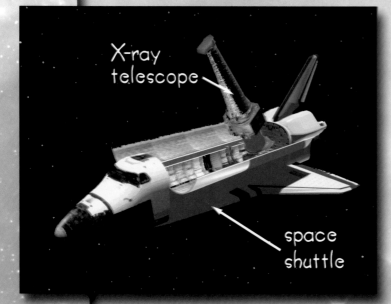

X-ray telescope

space shuttle

14

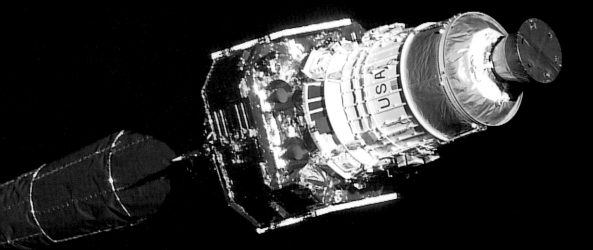

X-ray telescope, named *Chandra*

First, they tested the telescope. Next, they flipped some switches and let the telescope go into space. Then the telescope used its rockets to fly higher into space.

What does the X-ray telescope do?

a black hole

An X-ray telescope sees light that is too strong for our eyes. It sees gas and light being pulled into black holes.

an exploding star

The telescope sends important pictures back to Earth. These pictures show scientists new things in the universe.

17

Did the astronauts do other jobs, too?

* * * * * * * * * * *

plant experiment

Yes. They did experiments with plants and exercise machines. They were studying life without gravity.

✳✳✳✳✳✳✳✳✳✳✳✳ ✳✳✳✳✳✳✳✳✳

When there was some time to rest, the astronauts could look out their window. They saw Earth from many, many miles away!

Rocky Mountains in Colorado

Would you like to fly into space? ✳✳✳✳

Do you like math and science? Do you like to visit new places? Do you like fast roller coasters? Astronauts do, too! Maybe someday you will become an astronaut, just like Eileen Collins.

What is in your night sky?

You will need:
- ✔ journal
- ✔ pencil
- ✔ flashlight

1. Go outside at night with an adult. Look at the moon and the stars. Draw what you see. Ask questions like: What is the shape of the moon? What stars look brightest? Write about the night sky in your journal.

2. Watch the sky every night for a month. Do this at the same time each night. How does the sky change? How does it stay the same? Write down what you think in your journal.

The changing view of the moon

Learn More

Books

Bredeson, Carmen. *Astronauts*. New York: Children's Press, 2003.

Hayden, Kate. *Astronaut, Living in Space*. New York: Dorling Kindersley, 2000.

Mattern, Joanne. *Astronauts*. New York: The Rosen Publishing Group, Inc., 2002.

Murphy, Patricia J. *Why Does the Moon Change Its Face?* New York: The Rosen Publishing Group, Inc., 2003.

Shearer, Deborah A. *Astronauts at Work*. Mankato, Minn.: Capstone Press, Inc., 2002.

Web Sites

The Kennedy Space Center
<http://www.ksc.nasa.gov>

NASA Human Space Flight
<http://www.spaceflight.nasa.gov>

NASA Kids
<http://kids.msfc.nasa.gov>

Index

In memory of the space shuttle Columbia *crew*

Series Literacy Consultant:
Allan A. De Fina, Ph.D.
Past President of the New Jersey Reading Association
Professor, Department of Literacy Education

New Jersey City University
Science Consultant:
Marianne J. Dyson
Former NASA Flight Controller

Note to Teachers and Parents: The *I Like Science!* series supports the National Science Education Standards for K–4 science, including content standards "Science as a human endeavor" and "Science as inquiry." The Words to Know section introduces subject-specific vocabulary, including pronunciation and definitions. Early readers may require help with these new words.

Library of Congress Cataloging-in-Publication Data

Murphy, Patricia J., 1963–
    Exploring space with an astronaut / Patricia J. Murphy.
        p. cm. — (I like science!)
    Summary: Briefly explains the work of astronauts, scientists who travel on the space shuttle to study outer space and to conduct experiments.
    Includes index.
    ISBN-10: 0-7660-2268-4
    1. Astronautics—Juvenile literature. 2. Outer space—Exploration—Juvenile literature. [1. Astronautics. 2. Outer space—Exploration. 3. Astronauts.] I. Title. II. Series.
TL793.M837 2004
629.45-dc21   2003011116

ISBN-13: 978-0-7660-2268-3

Printed in the United States of America

10 9 8 7 6 5 4 3

To Our Readers: We have done our best to make sure all Internet Addresses in this book were active and appropriate when we went to press. However, the author and the publisher have no control over and assume no liability for the material available on those Internet sites or on other Web sites they may link to. Any comments or suggestions can be sent by e-mail to comments@enslow.com or to the address on the back cover.

Photo Credits: All photos courtesy of National Aeronautics and Space Administration (NASA), except p. 21 (U.S. Naval Observatory).

Cover Photo: NASA